Rhythm: Repeating segments of a design establishes a rhythm in the piece. It can be a certain flower which appears with regularity or possibly the repetition of an established shape. However, the repetition cannot be dull; there must be some excitement created by different elements yet this excitement must not harm the rhythmic flow.

Design Elements

Line, form, space, texture and color are elements within a design used and interpreted by the designer to give an individual look to the piece. Each designer will establish his or her own style, but these elements must always be incorporated.

Line: A visual path for the eye to follow through the arrangement is provided by establishing the lines within the design. A static line remains inside the form of the design just following the width, length or depth without providing any unusual movement within the design. A dynamic line provides continuous movement within a design; it is active and displays an unusual element, such as a curving line within a rectangular arrangement.

Form: The external appearance of a design is defined by the materials used, establishing the width, height and depth. A "closed form" is a solid, compact design. An "open form" has spreading and radiating parts with space between them.

Space: The area within the established design is space. *Positive space* is the area which is occupied by materials, either one piece or a mass of pieces. If the design consists of a mass of flowers with the entire design filling positive space, more emphasis is placed on the design shape or style instead of individual elements within the design. *Negative space* is the area between flowers in an open design. The unfilled negative space puts emphasis on the separate elements instead of the entire design.

Texture: Varying the types of materials used in a design adds interest. The viewer's eye stays within the design longer, exploring the changing textures. Even something as simple as using flowers with contrasting textures or ribbons and bases or containers with interesting textures makes a design more attractive, thereby increasing its textural interest.

Color: Usually the first element of a design to which people react is color. It can make or break a floral design! Silk flowers come in all different shades, tints, hues and tones of color. There are more restrictions in color blending with fresh flowers since they are available in particular colors. The color wheel is helpful in deciding which colors can be effectively used together.

Definitions of color: *Hue is* the full intensity of a color. *Tint* is the color with white added, *tone* is the color with grey added, and *shade* is the color with black added.

   Monochromatic colors are tints, shades and tones of one color.
   Analogous colors include one primary color and the adjacent colors within 90° on the color wheel.
   Complementary colors are two colors which lie directly across from each other on the color wheel.
   Triad colors are three colors equidistant from each other on the color wheel.
   Split complement colors are one hue combined with the color on each side of its direct complement.

Design Styles

In this book we have produced designs which fall within certain guidelines, defining the style of each. We have chosen to highlight the following design forms.

Symmetrical Triangle: A vertical center line or axis is present in the design with the two sides equal in shape. However, it's not necessary for the two sides to be mirror images or even contain the same materials, just for them to be visually equal.

Asymmetrical Triangle: Again, the vertical line or axis is established in a triangular design, but the sides aren't equal. One side has more material in it, becoming visually heavier than the other side.

Vertical: The entire design is very narrow and tall. The materials pull the viewer's eye up or down through the arrangement, with the various textures adding interest.

Horizontal: All the materials are kept within two horizontal parallel lines. As in the vertical design, the diversity of materials provides the excitement within the arrangement.

Circular: The components are kept within a circular shape, radiating out from a binding point. The individual elements can be tightly restrained or even in clusters within the circle.

Oval: The materials are kept within the oval shape, radiating outward from the binding point as with the circular design.

Crescent: The components are arranged to repeat a smooth circular motion. They generally stay within the crescent shape but can be intersected by other materials, bringing the viewer's eye back into the center of the design.

Hogarth Curve: A very graceful line is established in this relaxed "S" curve shape. Silk flowers are more easily shaped to fit this design whereas fresh materials must be chosen by their own shape to retain the gentle curved line.

Waterfall: Flowers and materials are presented as if they are cascading out of the container or base. To form a striking waterfall, the items are layered in place beginning with the underneath groups and building over them more and more layers of veiled material.

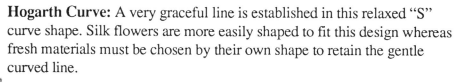

Vegetative: The components in the design are inserted as they would grow in nature. The design should look very natural, with a calming or peaceful feel to it. All flowers used must be used as they grow in nature.

Landscape: This style is similar to the vegetative, but on a larger scale. The materials are placed in the design as they would appear in a garden, but the human hand is present in the placement and the elements have a slightly "arranged" look.

Garden: Also similar to the vegetative and landscape, this style exhibits the look of a garden. The flowers are inserted as they would grow in a garden and the design can include grasses to make it look a bit wild.

"Interpretive" is a word which will be mentioned in a few designs. The design style has been followed to a certain degree, but the designer has chosen to include his or her own execution of the arrangement. For example, the circular wreath on pages 23 and 24 is interpretive because the designer did not produce a filled-in circular design. Instead, she chose to repeat the circular motion of the wreaths several times without filling the center area with flowers. The designer has control over how rigid or loose the criteria for each design is followed. The basic elements are still present, but the designer adds his/her personal interpretation.

Design Techniques

The following techniques are found in many of the floral designs in this book. They have been interpreted by the designer in his or her unique way.

Clustering: A greater impact is achieved when flowers, especially smaller flowers.are inserted into a design in a cluster. The whole cluster is viewed as a single unit with little or no air in between, maximizing the material colors, textures or shapes.

Banding: Adding an extra decoration to a design can be done by taping flowers or materials together. It is just for ornamentation and causes the viewer to focus on a particular flower. Raffia and ribbon are the most commonly used banding materials.

Framing: By placing tall, inward-curving materials around the outside of a design, the viewer's eye is brought back into the center or focal point of the arrangement. Many times the framing is done to emphasize the entire arrangement, but individual areas or flowers can be framed separately. Framing isolates and calls attention to the focal area of a composition.

Sheltering: This is done by inserting a tall, sometimes large, flower or plant material to extend above the focal area of the design. It shelters the smaller flowers which are down in the focal area. It also exists when the designer works within the confines of the diameter of the container as in a vertical design.

Parallelism: All the materials are placed in vertical lines in the design. The flowers can be grouped together, but space is left between the groups.

FLAT BOW

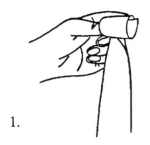

1.

1. Begin with one end of the ribbon and make a center loop the desired length. Twist the ribbon to keep the right side showing.

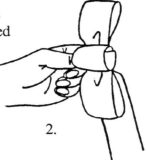

2.

2. Make a loop the specified length on one side of your thumb. Twist the ribbon and form a matching loop on the other side.

3.

3. Continue making loops of graduating sizes on each side of your thumb, positioning each just under the last loop, until the desired number is reached. For the tails, bring the ribbon end up and hold in place under the bow.

4.

4. Insert a wire length through the center loop. Bring the ends to the back, catching the ribbon end, and twist to secure. Cut the ribbon tails to the desired lengths, then trim each tail diagonally or in an inverted "V."

PUFFY BOW

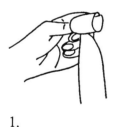

1.

1. If a center loop is required, begin with one end of the ribbon length and make the center loop. Twist the ribbon to keep the right side showing. If no center loop is called for, begin with step 2.

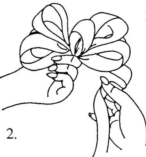

2.

2. Make a loop on one side of your thumb. Give the ribbon a twist and make another loop on the other side of your thumb. Continue making loops and twists until the desired number is reached (a ten-loop bow has five loops on each side), ending with a twist.

3.

3. For tails or additional long loops: Bring the end of the ribbon length up and hold at the back of the bow, making a long loop which can then be cut into tails.

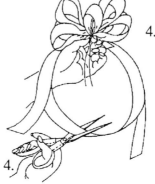

4.

4. Insert a wire through the center loop. Bring the ends to the back, being sure to catch the ribbon end, and twist securely. Cut the tails to the desired lengths or leave as long loops. Trim each tail diagonally or in an inverted "V."

1. Insert the soaked foam into the liner and the liner into the container.

2. Insert a 21" and a 13" stem of star gazer lilies into the foam center, establishing the height of the arrangement. Insert three 18" dendrobium orchids, one in the center extending upward, and one on each side, extending downward, establishing the triangular shape. Now insert another 18" orchid branch on each side between the upright and lower orchid branch.

3. Cut the berries off the eucalyptus and save. Cut eucalyptus branches the same length as the lilies and orchids. Insert them within the triangular line already established.

4. Cut 9"-12" stems of ting ting; save all the pieces. Wire the upper ends together in a cluster and insert it into the back of the foam angled to the left. Wire all the stems together, then attach them to a wood pick. Insert the pick into the foam front, allowing the stems to angle down-ward to the right. This diagonal line adds interest and flair to a rigid arrangement.

5. Insert the eucalyptus berries at the front to extend downward. Cut and insert the monte casino as the orchids were in step 2. Cut the remaining into a 9" and a 12" stem, and insert them to extend forward in the design.

6. Use the ribbon to make three 5" loops and four 6"-8" tails; attach them to a wood pick. Insert the pick just above the eucalyptus berries.

LILIES IN TERRA COTTA
symmetrical triangle style, fresh flowers
photo on page 6

12" tall square terra cotta container and liner
2 stems of white star gazer lilies
5 stems of white dendrobium orchids
6-8 stems of willow eucalyptus with berries
6 stems of monte casino
1 oz. of dark green ting ting
1³/₄ yards of #9 ivy wired Bedford
    Bendable™ ribbon
floral foam for fresh flowers,
    soaked in water
4" long wired wood picks
30-gauge wire

Designer Tip:
• When using willow eucalyptus with berries in an arrangement, remove the berry clusters, attach to picks and insert separately for added texture and interest.

LILIES IN TERRA COTTA
by Rich Salvaggio, AIFD, aaf

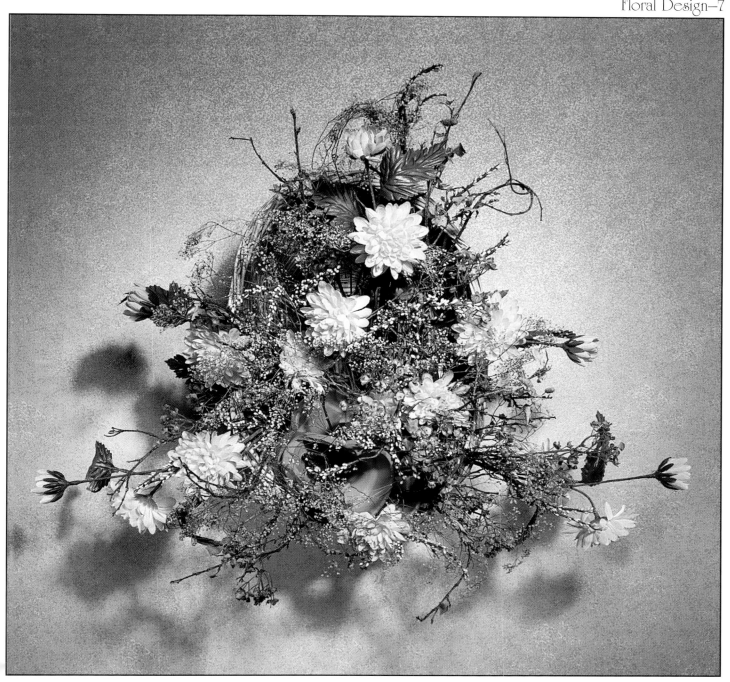

BASKET WITH CLAY POTS
by Teresa Nelson

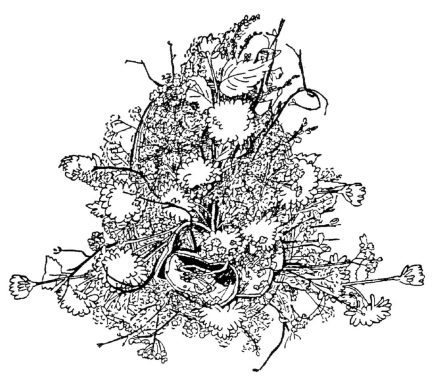

BASKET WITH CLAY POTS

symmetrical triangle style, silk flowers
photo on page 7

13"x9"x5" oval basket
three 4" terra cotta flower pots, hammer
6 stems of yellow silk chrysanthemums, each
*   with two 2¹/₂" wide blossoms and a bud*
6 stems of white silk berries, each with a 12"
*   section of 4"-6" long berry sprigs*
5 stems of burgundy silk baby's breath,
*   each with three 10" sprigs of many ¹/₄"*
*   wide blossoms*
2 oz. of birch twigs, 8"-16" long
1 oz. of natural dried baby's breath
¹/₄ oz. of sheet moss
4"x3"x2" block of floral foam for silks
serrated knife
U-shaped floral pins
6" of 24-gauge wire (for a hanger)
glue gun and sticks

1. Attach a wire loop hanger to the upper back of the basket. Cut the foam to fit the inside bottom of the basket and glue in place. Cut away the front left corner of the foam to fit a pot, spilling over the front basket edge. Cover the foam with moss and secure with U-pins.

2. Break the pots with the hammer and arrange them to spill over the front basket edge, angling from left to right. Glue U-pins to the back of them and insert into the foam; glue them to each other for added security.

3. Cut a mum stem to 16" and insert it into the foam center to extend upright. Cut two 15" stems; insert one into each side of the foam, angling outward and establishing the triangle. Cut two stems to 11"; insert one into each side of the foam at a 45° to fill in the triangle sides. Cut the last stem into 6" single flower sprigs and insert around the pots at the lower front to fill empty spaces.

4. Cut a 17" berry stem and insert it near the upright mum. Cut two 13" stems and insert one near each 15" mum. Cut the remaining stems into 6"-8" sprigs; insert them evenly spaced among the lower mums.

5. Insert the twigs into the foam near flowers of similar lengths, with some extending forward, out the basket. Cut the silk baby's breath into 6"-14" sprigs; insert them into the foam near flowers of similar lengths. Repeat with the dried baby's breath.

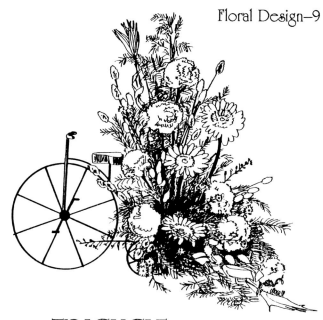

1. Poke two holes into the top of the liner and wire it to the back of the tricycle. Insert the soaked foam into the liner.
2. Insert galax leaves around the foam sides to hide the container.
3. Insert four carnations, 18", 14", 10" and 6", upright into the foam, stair-stepping them in a vertical line, yet allowing them to angle slightly away from the line. Insert an 11" carnation horizontally to the right. Insert a 9" and an 8" carnation angled above it.
4. Insert a 14" gerbera between the vertical and horizontal carnations, angled slightly right. Insert a 9" in front of it and a 3" stem in front of that one.
5. Braid two emerald fern leaves (see the Designer Tip, right). Insert one beside the tallest carnation and one to extend from under the longest horizontal carnation.
6. Insert monte casino sprigs among all the flowers to add a light and whimsical feeling to the design. Add more galax leaves and 6" mingeri fern sprigs to cover the foam.
7. Attach 4-6 sprigs of phalaris together to a wood pick to make a cluster. Insert seven clusters among the flowers of similar lengths, spacing them evenly in the design.

TRICYCLE

asymmetrical triangle style, fresh flowers
photo on page 10

12" tall wrought iron tricycle
3 stems of apple blossom gerbera daisies
7 stems of white carnations
2 stems of emerald fern
2 stems of mingeri fern
1 stem of monte casino
2 oz. of coral dried phalaris grass
12 galax leaves
1 yard of gold spaghetti wired Bedford
   Bendable™ ribbon
3"x2" tall plastic liner
floral foam for fresh flowers, soaked in water
4" long wired wood picks
30-gauge wire

Designer Tip:
• To braid emerald fern leaves: Bend the lowest leaf from each side of the stem over the top of the stem, overlapping them. Repeat with the next leaf on each side, basket-weaving them next to the first two. Repeat with the third set, again weaving them among the first four leaves. Pinch the leaf ends next to the stem and wrap with wired ribbon to hold. Repeat again with the next three sets of leaves and wire to hold near the end of the branch. Coil the ribbon ends decoratively around a pen or pencil.

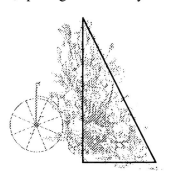

TRICYCLE
by Rich Salvaggio, AIFD, aaf

BIRDHOUSE
by TeresaNelson

BIRDHOUSE

asymmetrical triangle style, silk flowers
photo on page 11

15" tall rattan birdhouse
two 4" long peach mushroom birds
2¹/₄ yards of 1¹/₂" wide peach moire ribbon
6 stems of peach silk roses, each with a 3"-4"
*   wide blossom and many leaves*
1 green silk Swedish ivy bush with two 20"
*   and three 14" branches*
3 stems of grey/mauve berries, each with a
*   14" section of ³/₈" wide berries*
2 stems of white silk daisies, each with three
*   12" sprigs of ³/₄" wide blossoms*
2 oz. of natural dried linum flax
18-gauge wire, green floral tape
8" of 24-gauge wire (for the bow)
4"x4"x2" block of floral foam for silk flowers
¹/₄ oz. of sheet moss
U-shaped floral pins
glue gun and sticks

1. Glue the foam inside the birdhouse near one corner; cover with moss and secure with U-pins. Cut two roses to 18"; insert one upright in the foam to extend through the roof at the left side. Insert the other into the right side of the foam to extend right and downward.

2. Cut two roses to 12"; insert one just right of the upper rose, angled right. Insert one above the lower rose, angled upward. Cut two roses to 9"; insert one in front of the upright rose and one at the right front corner of the birdhouse.

3. Cut each daisy stem into three sprigs. Floral tape 18-gauge wire to the stems of four sprigs. Cut two sprigs to 18", two to 12" and two to 10". Insert daisy sprigs near roses of the same lengths.

4. Use the ribbon to make a puffy bow (see page 4) with a center loop, eight 3" loops a 7" and a 10" tail. Insert the wire stem into the lower front of the foam.

5. Cut two 19" ivy branches; insert one near each 18" rose. Cut two 13" ivy branches; insert one behind the upright 9" rose and one into the lower right front of the foam. Cut the last branch into 5"-6" sprigs; insert one just left of the bow and the rest into the foam around the back.

6. Cut two berry stems to 16"; insert one near each 18" rose at similar angles. Cut the last berry stem into 7"-10" sprigs; insert them evenly spaced around the bow. Cut the flax into 8"-20" sprigs. Insert them evenly spaced into the foam near flowers of similar lengths. Glue one bird in the bow center and the other on the roof at the right.

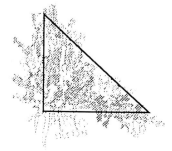

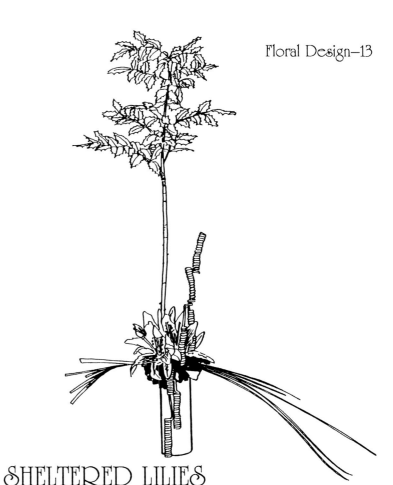

1. Follow the manufacturer's directions to cover and seal the vase with Fleck Stone™. Glue three cane springs to the vase front, extending downward as shown. Soak the foam and insert it into the vase.

2. Square the Oregon grape stem and insert upright into the left side of the foam. Insert galax leaves around the vase rim, making a collar to hide the foam.

3. Insert four cane springs upright into the foam; the shortest is 5" and the stems graduate up to 15" tall.

4. Cut the lower 8"-12" off the bear grass; save all the pieces. Wire the stems together near the upper end and insert horizontally into the left side of the foam. Wire the stems of the upper pieces together and insert horizontally into the right side of the foam.

5. Cut the lily blossoms with 3" stems; insert them in a cluster around the grape and cane spring stems. Begin with the front and lowest blossom, continuing back on the left and right.

SHELTERED LILIES

vertical with the sheltering technique, fresh flowers
photo on page 14

36" stem of Oregon grape
2 stems of star gazer lilies with 7 blossoms
    and buds
10 stems of bear grass
8 galax leaves
7 stems of blue metallic cane springs
24-gauge wire
12" tall green cylinder vase (from Lomey)
ironstone Fleck Stone™ paint kit
floral foam for fresh flowers, soaked in water
glue gun and sticks

Designer Tip:
• For very tall materials, cut the stem square for about 6" to ensure that it stays in place when inserted into the foam; insert the stem as far as possible into the foam. The tallest piece is always the first insertion in a vertical design, establishing the height. The Oregon grape serves as a "sheltering" device, protecting the lower portion of the arrangement.

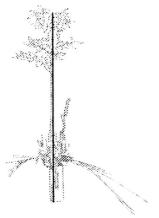

SHELTERED LILIES
by Rich Salvaggio, AIFD, aaf

SPRING BUNDLE
by Teresa Nelson

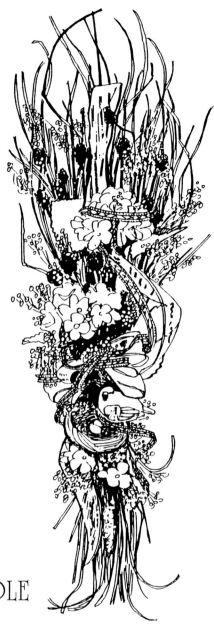

SPRING BUNDLE

vertical style, silk flowers
photo on page 15

36" TWIGS™ broom (used upside down)
2 stems of lavender silk hydrangea, each
  with a 4" wide cluster of blossoms
2 oz. of purple dried starburst flowers
1 oz. of natural dried baby's breath
2³/₄ yards of 1¹/₂" wide purple/lavender/
  brown sheer ribbon
2³/₄ yards of ³/₈" wide gold mesh wired
  ribbon
3" bird nest
three ³/₄" speckled eggs
3" long blue/mauve mushroom bird
small handful of American Moss® grey
  excelsior
24-gauge wire
hot glue gun and sticks

1. Cut one hydrangea to 15" and one to 10". Wire them to the front of the broom, extending upward.
2. Thread a piece of wire into the nest from one side then back out; wrap the wire ends around the lower front of the broom over the hydrangea stems and twist them at the back. Glue the moss in the nest, then glue the eggs on top of it.
3. Hold the gold ribbon over the sheer ribbon and handle as one. Make a puffy bow (see page 4) with a center loop, eight 3" loops, a 12" and a 20" tail. Glue it to the broom front slightly left and above the nest. Glue the bird to the back rim of the nest.
4. Cut the starburst into 6"-10" sprigs. Glue the longer sprigs behind the upper hydrangea with the rest around the lower hydrangea.
5. Cut a 6-blossom hydrangea off the back side of the tallest hydrangea and glue it under the nest. Cut 2"-4" starburst sprigs; glue them under the nest extending downward around the hydrangea blossoms and the bow.
6. Cut and glue the baby's breath as the starburst was in step 4. Tuck the two long ribbon tails among the upper twigs and flowers; tuck the shorter tails among the twigs under the nest. Attach a wire loop hanger to the back.

1. Cut the foam to fit the liner, allowing it to extend 1" above the basket edge. Glue the soaked foam into the liner.
2. Wire a 20" twig branch along the front of the basket rim, keeping it horizontal. Wire a 24" branch behind the first to curve around the basket front; be sure to wire the branch tips in place to secure them horizontally. Add in 12"–16" branches among the first two to fill in the empty spaces.
3. Insert the eucalyptus branches to extend among the twigs, helping to establish the horizontal line. Insert 5"–6" fern sprigs among the twigs to cover the foam, always inserting them horizontally, even in the top of the foam. This creates "ground cover" while still adhering to the horizontal design.
4. Follow the directions in the Designer Tip, right, to insert two cattleya orchids into the left side of the basket. Insert the third orchid into the water tube, then glue three 4" wood picks around it and insert it behind the other two orchids.
5. Insert 18", 17" and 15" branches of white dendrobium orchids to extend over the right edge of the basket above the twigs. Cut another branch into an 8" and a 12" sprig. Insert the 12" sprig in front of the long orchid stems and the 8" sprig at an angle just right of the large orchids.
6. To pull the white color over to the left side of the design, insert four 6"–11" sprigs of monte casino into the left end of the foam. Make six 3"–6" concentric circles of ribbon and wire to hold; insert them into the left end of the foam. Coil more ribbon back and forth four times along the horizontal line of the design; attach the ends to the twigs.

TWIG BASKET ARRANGEMENT
horizontal style, fresh flowers
photo on page 18

12"x9" oval twig basket with a 12" tall handle
20"–24" curving twig branches pulled from a wreath
5 branches of white dendrobium orchids
3 large white cattleya orchids with yellow lips
5 branches of willow eucalyptus
1 stem of monte casino
1 stem of ming fern
6 yards of spaghetti opalescent wired Bedford Bendable™ ribbon
plastic liner for the basket
floral foam for fresh flowers, soaked in water
4" long wired wood picks
5" water tube
30-gauge wire

Designer Tip:
• Because orchids are not to be inserted directly into foam, first make a hole in the foam with a pencil. Wire a wood pick to the orchid stem and insert it beside the hole so the stem is in the hole. This allows the orchid stem to draw enough water, since the hole will fill first as the arrangement is watered. When an orchid needs to extend higher into the arrangement, leave it in the water tube and glue picks directly to the tube. The picks are then inserted into the foam, raising the tube and orchid up into the arrangement.

TWIG BASKET ARRANGEMENT
by Rich Salvaggio, AIFD, aaf

RANUNCULA AND TWIG SWAG
by Teresa Nelson

1. Cut the ranunculas to these lengths: 8", two 12", two 16" and two 18" sprigs. Wire them across the front of the swag, one of each length on each end. Position them as shown in the photo.
2. Use the ribbon to make a flat bow (see page 4) with a center loop, two 3$\frac{1}{2}$" loops, two 5" loops, and two 25" tails. Glue it to angle across the front of the swag, then tuck a tail among the twigs on each end.
3. Cut the fern into 8"-18" sprigs. Glue them evenly spaced among the flowers, locating the shorter sprigs near the shorter flowers and the longer sprigs near the longer flowers.
4. Cut 10"-14" koolseed sprigs; glue them evenly spaced among the flowers and fern. Repeat with the caspia.
5. Cut 5" sprigs of caspia, koolseed and fern; glue them evenly spaced around and among the bow loops.
6. Attach a wire loop hanger to the back.

RANUNCULA AND TWIG SWAG

horizontal style, silk flowers
photo on page 19

40" TWIGS™ swag
2³/₄ yards of 2¹/₂" wide gold/rose metallic ribbon
8 stems of dark mauve silk ranunculas
3 oz. of preserved asparagus fern
4 oz. of natural dried koolseed
3 oz. of maroon dried caspia
30-gauge wire
8" of 24-gauge wire (for bow)
hot glue gun and sticks

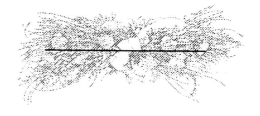

1. Glue the soaked foam into the container.
2. Cut a 4" long heavy Y-shaped branch. Insert it through the underside of the wreath with the "Y" pointing downward. Hook the crotch over the lip of the container, with the wreath back resting on the back of the container rim; glue in place.
3. Wire 15 bear grass stems together into a bundle. Insert into the foam on the left extending to the right front. Repeat with three more bundles, inserting them around the front of the foam. Wire together the ends of the two left bundles together, fanning out the strands. Bring these strands over to the next bundle and wire, again fanning the strands. Repeat, bringing the strands from the first three bundles to the last one. This creates circular motion within the design.
4. Insert galax leaves around the edge of the container to hide it from view. Cut 8"–10" mingeri sprigs and insert them horizontally into the foam to cover it and the bowl; angle the fern out into the wreath twigs to bring color to them.
5. Insert a 24" orchid branch into the left side of the foam, curving it around to the right and hooking the florets among the bear grass to hold it in place. Insert one over each bear grass cluster. Insert one on each side near the foam back extending upward; bring the ends together and wrap the buds around each other, creating a circle.
6. Insert a 24" heather stem on each side of the foam behind the upright orchids; repeat with 21" stems in front of the orchids. Twist the ends together as with the orchids.
7. Insert a 20" rose behind the tallest heather circle, angled left. Insert a 12" rose in front of the small heather circle, angled forward. Insert four more roses among the circles, all angled left and near the wreath left side.
8. Insert short heather sprigs to fill any empty spaces at the base of the foam.

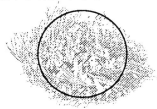

TWIGGY WREATH

circular style, fresh flowers
photo on page 22

28" round twig wreath (from Colorado
   Evergreen Import Co.)
$^1/_2$ bunch of bear grass
7 hot pink roses
7 variegated dendrobium orchids
$^1/_3$ bunch mauve heather
15 galax leaves
1 bunch of mingeri fern sprigs
$9^1/_2$"x6" round plastic container
floral foam for fresh flowers, soaked in
   water
30-gauge wire
hot glue gun and sticks

Designer Tips:
• Elevating the back of the wreath keeps this design from looking flat and two-dimensional.
• Make sure the orchids are pliable near the ends before inserting them into the design.

TWIGGY WREATH
by Rich Salvaggio, AIFD, aaf

WREATH OF POPPIES
by Teresa Nelson

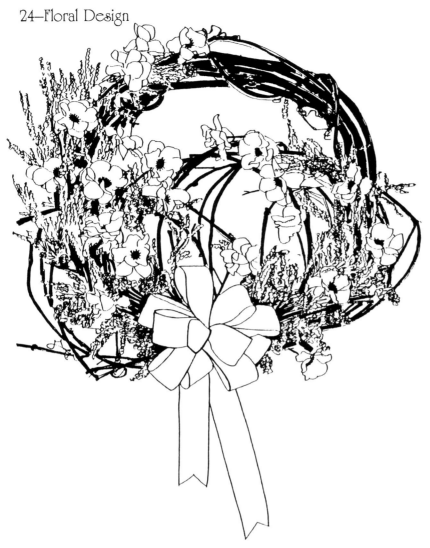

WREATH OF POPPIES

circular style, silk flowers
photo on page 23

18" grapevine wreath
12" grapevine wreath
4 stems of purple/cream silk poppies, each
  with three 2" wide blossoms
3 stems of mauve silk poppies, each with
  three 2" wide blossoms
3 stems of lavender silk maize, each with a
  15" section of feathery sprigs
2 oz. of purple preserved statice sinuata
3 1/4 yards of purple/brown 1³/₄" wide printed
  ribbon
30-gauge wire
8" of 24-gauge wire (for the bow)
glue gun and sticks

1. Separate the small wreath vines and spread them across the lower area of the large wreath; wire to secure.
2. Cut a mauve poppy stem to 18" and curve it to follow the curve on the right side of a small wreath section; wire. Cut a 12" purple poppy and wire in front of the first one. Cut another to 9" and wire in front of the last.
3. Cut a purple poppy stem to 15" and wire to curve over the left side of a small wreath section. Cut a mauve poppy to 11" and wire in front of it.
4. Cut a purple poppy stem to 19"; wire to curve over the left side of the large wreath. Cut a 15" purple poppy and wire in front of the 19" poppy.
5. Use the ribbon to make a puffy bow (see page 4) with a center loop, ten 4" loops, a 9" and a 12" tail. Glue as shown.
6. Wire a maize stem among the poppies on the left side of the large wreath. Cut a stem to 15" and wire among the flowers on the right side of the small wreath. Cut the last stem into an 11" and an 8" sprig. Glue the 11" sprig to curve over the left side of the small wreath. Glue the 8" sprigs over the lower stem area of the poppies on the large wreath.
7. Cut the statice into 6"-8" sprigs; glue them evenly spaced among all the flowers. Cut six 3"-4" sprigs and glue around the bow.
8. Attach a wire loop hanger to the back.

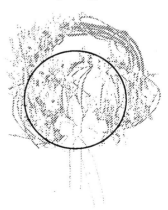

1. Follow the manufacturer's directions to cover and seal the plastic bowl with Fleck Stone™. Glue the soaked foam into the bowl horizontally. Insert a collar of galax leaves around the front of the foam to hide it.
2. Pin a cluster of grapes into the left front of the foam to extend over the bowl front.
3. Attach five 36" strands of bear grass to a wood pick and insert into one side of the foam at 45°. Repeat on the other side. Bring the grass ends together over the center of the arrangement and secure together with a 1" length of wire. Wrap and tie a bear grass stem over the wire to hide it.
4. Insert the curly willow branches upright into the foam center. Insert one orchid at the lower right front of the bowl; insert the other above and left of the first, leaving it in the water vial (see Designer Tip, page 17.)
5. Strip the lower leaves off an emerald fern—all but the upper 2–4 leaves. Hold the stripped leaves together; attach them to a wood pick. Insert them behind the upper orchid and right of the willow. Repeat with the other fern stem. Cut one fern stem to 21" and one to 14"; insert them horizontally into the right side of the foam.
6. Spray the grapes and fern stems with the gloss spray.

IRONSTONE BOWL
oval style, fresh flowers
photo on page 26

11 strands of bear grass
1 cluster of red grapes
2 white cattleya orchids with purple lips
three 26" curly willow branches
2 stems of emerald fern
12" round grey plastic bowl (from Lomey)
ironstone Fleck Stone™ paint kit
leaf gloss spray
30-gauge wire
U-shaped floral pins
4" long wired wood picks
floral foam for fresh flowers, soaked in
    water
glue gun and sticks

Designer Tip:
• When using grapes, spraying with leaf gloss or a light glitter spray creates a wonderful iridescent shine. Make sure the recipient is notified not to eat the treated grapes!

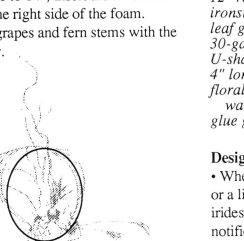

IRONSTONE BOWL by Rich Salvaggio, AIFD, aaf

IVY AND AZALEA
WREATH
by Teresa Nelson

IVY AND AZALEA WREATH

oval style, silk flowers
photo on page 27

18" wide TWIGS™ wreath
1 variegated silk English ivy vine with three 30" and three 21" branches
1 white silk azalea bush with eleven 9"-16" branches
3 stems of mauve silk baby's breath, each with four 8"-10" sprigs of many ³/₈" wide blossoms
8 stems of burgundy dried silk rosebuds, each with a sprig of five 1" wide blossoms
1¹/₂ yards of 2¹/₂" wide burgundy/green wire-edged ribbon
¹/₂ oz. of sheet moss
8"x1"x3" block of floral foam for silks
30-gauge wire
U-shaped floral pins
8" of 24-gauge wire (for bow)
white spray paint
hot glue gun and sticks

1. Lightly spray the wreath with white paint. Cut the foam to fit the inside bottom of the wreath, cover it with moss and wire it in place.

2. Cut two 30" ivy sprigs. Insert them into the left end of the foam, then wire them to curve over the top of the wreath. Cut the remaining 30" ivy branch into three 10" sprigs and set them aside. Cut one 21" ivy branch and two 18" branches. Insert the 21" branch into the lower center of the foam to extend downward, then insert an 18" branch on each side of it.

3. Cut the azalea branches off the main stem. Insert an 11" stem into the top of the foam and one to extend downward. Insert an 8" stem to extend out toward each side. Fill in the empty areas around the sides and in the center front with the remaining stems, cutting them to stay within the oval shape.

4. Use the ribbon to make a flat bow (see page 4) with a center loop, two 4¹/₂" loops, a 12" and a 14" tail. Insert it into the lower center of the foam, tucking the tails among the lower ivy.

5. Cut the rose stems into 8"-11" lengths. Insert them evenly spaced near the azaleas of the same lengths, following the oval shape.

6. Cut the baby's breath into 6"-11" sprigs and insert as the roses were in step 5.

7. Insert the three 10" ivy sprigs evenly spaced among the upper flowers.

8. Attach a wire loop hanger to the back.

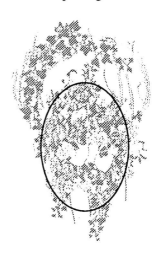

1. Glue the foam into the saucer; trim the corners to make a dome.

2. Square the bottom of a birch twig and dip into pan glue; insert into the left side of the foam to curve up over the top. Repeat with two shorter pieces, inserting them into the opposite side of the foam, creating a crescent framing line.

3. Strip the foliage and all but one blossom and a bud off a stem of lilies, saving all the blossoms. Cut it to 19" and insert into the foam center. Strip the second lily stem down to two blossoms and cut it to 9"; insert in front of the first. Insert the stripped blossoms clustered around the stems.

4. Cut the carnations to 3"–9" lengths. Insert in a cluster just left of the lilies, giving depth to the arrangement.

5. Cut one stem of emerald fern to 16" and one to 10"; strip off all but the two end leaves of each, saving the leaves. Insert the stems into the left of the foam following the curving twigs. Hold all the leaves from one fern stem together and attach to a wood pick. Insert into the foam between the lilies and carnations, making sure that the ends are in the foam to draw water.

6. Insert a 19" heather stem into the left of the foam following the curving twigs; insert a 16" stem into the right. This heather will reinforce the crescent framing lines of the twigs. Insert a 16" and a 13" heather stem side by side among the upright lilies in the center of the foam.

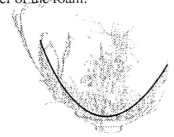

ORIENTAL SAUCER

crescent style, fresh flowers
photo on page 30

2 stems of star gazer lilies
8 stems of pink heather
6 stems of pink carnations
2 stems of emerald fern
curved twigs from a birch wreath
12" wide round bronze plastic saucer
floral foam for fresh flowers, soaked in
  water
4" long wired wood picks
hot glue pan and pellets

Designer Tips:
• Squaring a heavy stem before inserting it into foam will keep it from twisting or moving around as the design is being transported.
• All the stems of heather repeat the circular motion of the container and birch twigs, bringing the viewer's eye back into the arrangement.

ORIENTAL BOWL DESIGN
by Rich Salvaggio, AIFD, aaf

BIRD AND BERRIES
ON BARK
by Teresa Nelson

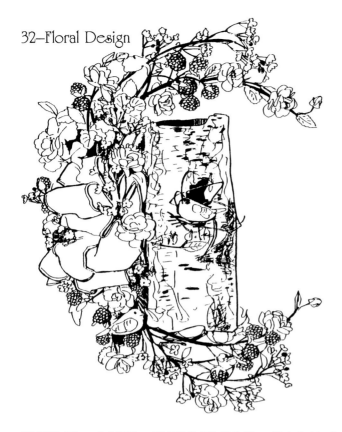

BIRD AND BERRIES ON BARK

crescent style, silk flowers
photo on page 31

two 2" mauve/grey mushroom birds
8"-10" tall tube of birch bark
4 stems of pink silk wild roses, each with
    four 1½" wide blossoms and a bud
3 stems of red/green silk blackberries, each
    with 2 sprigs of five ³/₄" wide berries
3 stems of burgundy silk baby's breath,
    each with four 8" sprigs of many ¹/₄"
    wide blossoms
1³/₄ yards of 2¹/₂" wide green/mauve/silver
    wire-edged sheer ribbon
1 Smithers-Oasis mini-deco holder
¹/₄ oz. of American Moss® grey excelsior
26-gauge wire
hot glue gun and sticks

1. If there isn't a hole in the bark, break one with your fingers for a natural look. Make the hole large enough to hold the bird just above the center in the front of the bark. If there isn't a hole in the bark, break one with your fingers for a natural look.

2. Glue the mini-deco holder to the center left of the bark.

3. Cut two 16" wild rose stems. Insert one into the top of the foam to curve over the top of the bark and to the right side. Repeat with the other one curving around the bottom of the bark and up the right side.

4. Cut two 12" berry stems, curve them to follow the same lines as the roses, and insert in front of the roses. Be sure they curve among the rose blossoms naturally.

5. Cut two 15" baby's breath stems. Insert one into the top and one into the bottom, both curving around to the right side of the bark.

6. Use the ribbon to make a puffy bow (see page 4) with a center loop, six 2³/₄" loops and two 6" tails. Wire and glue it to the front of the foam, to the left of the bark.

7. Cut each of the remaining two rose stems into a 4" and an 8" sprig. Insert an 8" sprig into the top of the foam, and one into the bottom of the foam, making sure they curve in the crescent shape.

8. Insert a 4" sprig in front of the bow, and one just behind.

9. Cut the third berry stem into a 4" and a 6" sprig. Insert the 6" sprig into the bottom of the foam shaping the berries to curve among the flowers, and the 4" sprig into the foam just behind the top of the bow.

10. Cut the last baby's breath stem into four 5"-6" sprigs. Insert them equally spaced around the bow.

11. Glue a tuft of moss at the bottom of the hole and glue a bird on top of it. Glue the second bird onto a berry near the bottom left edge of the bark. Glue any leftover moss to cover the foam around the back side and tuck it among the stems.

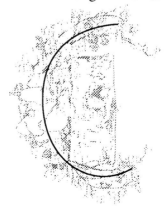

LOG BASKET

Hogarth curve style, fresh flowers
photo on page 34

1. Lightly spray the basket with gold paint, allowing the bark to show through. Insert the foam into the liner. Place the liner in the basket; surround it with moss to completely hide the liner and pull tufts of moss between the twigs.
2. Insert a 20" larkspur stem into the lower right of the foam to extend downward. Insert a 24" stem into the upper left of the foam to extend 45° toward the left.
3. Insert two orchids in front of each larkspur to reinforce the line established. Insert the fifth orchid angled to the lower left.
4. Add five Dutch iris stems, following and strengthening the lines established. Cut and insert fern among the flowers to fill and hide the mechanics; this will also add a lightness to the arrangement.
5. Cut and insert yellow mums into the foam, again following the lines of the design, to add depth to the arrangement. Cut and insert wheat among the flowers to extend the lines and bring the purple color back into the design.
6. Insert galax leaves around the back of the foam to cover it and the liner.

18" tall round log basket
2 stems of pink larkspur
5 stems of white dendrobium orchids
2 stems of spider mums each with 4-5 blossoms
4 stems of mingeri fern
5 stems of Dutch iris
8 galax leaves
3 oz. of lavender dried wheat
17¹/₂" tall round liner
floral foam for fresh flowers, soaked in water
gold spray paint
sheet moss

Designer Tips:
• Strip off the budded laterals from the stems of the larkspur. After establishing the line with the blossoming stems, insert the budded stems among them; these add softness to the design and will continue to open and bloom for about ten days in the arrangement.
• When using an open basket, insert stems through the openings; if not, the stems would extend too far forward or backward in the design.
• When inserting stems into a curved design, insert all of them to follow the initial curve first established, reinforcing the line.

LOG BASKET
by Rich Salvaggio, AIFD, aaf

SUNFLOWERS WALL BASKET
by Teresa Nelson

SUNFLOWERS WALL BASKET

Hogarth curve style, silk flowers
photo on page 34

13"x13"x7" wall basket
3 yards of 2¹/₂" wide gold/bronze satin
pleated, wire-edged ribbon
2 frosted fruit picks, each with a 1¹/₂" rust
apple, two 1" blue and burgundy plums,
a pine cone and 6 berries
1 plum pick with two 2" brownish
burgundy plums
6 stems of gold silk sunflowers, each with
two 4" wide blossoms, 2 buds, and a
dead blossom
5 stems of burgundy silk berries, each with
an 11" section of many ¹/₄" wide berries
3 oz. of peach dried heather
four 9"-11" pheasant feathers
1 oz. of sheet moss
gold and copper spray paints
4" long wired wood picks
U-shaped floral pins
two 8"x4"x3" blocks of floral foam for silks
22-gauge wire
hot glue gun and sticks

1. Lightly spray the basket gold; let dry then spray it copper, allowing some of the basket to show through. Cut the foam blocks to fit into the left side of the basket, extending 1" above the rim.
2. Cut two 22" sunflower stems; insert one into the top of the foam extending upward at the back and curving right. Insert the other into the foam front extending to the right over the basket, then curving left.
3. Cut two sunflower stems into 6"-14" sprigs and insert them into the foam top to curve among the first stem. Repeat with the remaining 2 stems, inserting them to curve among the lower sunflower stem. Arrange the flowers to follow the Hogarth curve that was established by the first two stems.
4. Use the ribbon to make a puffy bow (see page 4) with a center loop, six 4¹/₂" loops, a 24" and a 15" tail. Attach it to a wood pick and then insert into the foam between the upper and lower sunflowers.
5. Insert the plum pick into the foam in front of the bow center; insert one fruit pick on each side of it. Attach each feather to a wood pick; insert two among the upper flowers and two among the lower ones, all following the established curve and at varying heights.
6. Cut two berry stems to 18". Insert one among the upper and one among the lower flowers, again staying within the curve established by the sunflowers. Cut each remaining berry stem into two 8"-10" sprigs. Insert three among the upper flowers and three among the lower ones, all following the curve.
7. Cut the dried heather into 5"-18" sprigs. Insert them evenly spaced near flowers of similar lengths with the shortest sprigs around the fruit and bow.
8. Attach a wire loop hanger to the back.

3. Spray the trunk, ball and twigs with metallic copper paint. When dry, fill the basket with moss.

4. Soak the igloo in water, dry the bottom and glue it to the top of the ball. Insert a collar of galax leaves around the igloo edges to hide it.

5. Insert mingeri fern stems into the foam to follow the curve of the wreath branches. Insert monte casino among the fern, again following the curve.

6. Insert the oncidium orchid branches among all the monte casino and fern to follow the waterfall already established. Cut a single cymbidium orchid and insert it into the left of the foam. Cut a double orchid sprig with a 5" stem and insert it upright into the foam; cut the last sprig with a 2" stem and insert into the front.

7. Hold the cording and ribbon together and handle as one. Make a series of four loops of each, varying from 4" to 15" long; wire it to a wood pick and insert into the left of the foam. Repeat to make another set, varying from 14"-30" long; insert it into the right of the foam to "fall" among the flowers. Make a third set of four 5"-7" loops of each and insert into the top of the foam to extend upward and slightly right. Wrap the basket with cording and ribbon held together and tie in front, leaving the tails 6" long. Make a loopy bow (see page 4) with six 4"-5"loops and 6" tails; use the tails from the wrapping ribbons to tie the bow to the front of the basket.

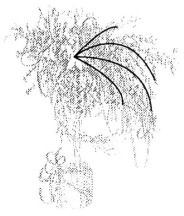

TWIG TOPIARY

waterfall style, fresh flowers
photo on page 38

18" birch wreath
2' tall twig topiary with base
5 branches of mingeri fern (from Nyren Brothers, Clifton Park, NY)
5 branches of burgundy oncidium orchids (from The Orchid Man)
1 branch of mauve cymbidium orchids (from The Orchid Man)
3 stems of monte casino
metallic copper and dark green spray paints
Oasis™ igloo for fresh flowers
green sheet moss
10-15 galax leaves
12 yards of cream satin twisted cord
12 yards of $^5/_8$" wide gold mesh wired ribbon
4"long wired wood picks
glue gun and sticks

Designer Tip:
• When creating a waterfall design, layer is place over layer repeatedly until the textured softness of the waterfall is achieved.

1. Spray the basket with dark green paint. Before dry, spray again with metallic copper paint, allowing some green areas to show through. Let dry.

2. Take the wreath apart carefully. Wire a long branch to the ball at the lower left. Wire three short branches at the top of the ball, with all the branches curving around the ball in the same direction and angling back into the ball itself.

TWIG TOPIARY by Rich Salvaggio, AIFD, aaf

TWIG SHELF WITH FLOWERS
by Teresa Nelson

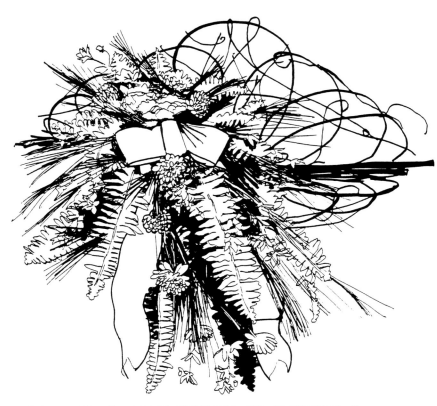

TWIG SHELF WITH FLOWERS

waterfall style, silk flowers
photo on page 39

two 32" long TWIGS® door crowns
1¹/₄ yards of 2³/₄" wide burgundy/green print wire-edged ribbon
6 stems of burgundy dried silk chrysanthemums, each with two 2¹/₂"-3" wide blossoms
3 stems of white silk chickweed, each with 4 sprigs of four 1¹/₂" wide blossoms
1 stem of mauve/cream/green silk ornamental cabbage
1 green silk Boston fern bush with twenty-four 8"-19" fronds
1 oz. of burgundy dried barba bode grass
1 oz. of American Moss® grey excelsior
4" wired wood picks
24-gauge wire (for bow), 30-gauge wire
18-gauge wire (for stems)
U-shaped floral pins
block of floral foam for silks
green floral tape
glue gun and sticks

1. Position the two door crowns together at a 90° with the horizontal bars matching; use 30-gauge wire to secure, making a shelf with a backdrop. On the shelf, trim away the outer 3¹/₂" in the center to reduce the shelf depth. Cover all sides of the foam with moss; wire it to the shelf near the left end.

2. The waterfall is made by layering materials, beginning with the longest pieces on the bottom and building layer upon layer with alternating materials. Cut the barba bode into 12"-20" stems and attach to wood picks, two stems to each pick.

3. Cut each chickweed stem into four sprigs; floral tape each to 18-gauge wire. Cut two to 19" and the rest into 10"-14" sprigs. Cut each mum into a single flower sprig and attach each to stem wire with floral tape. Cut two to 18" and the rest into 6"-15" sprigs. Cut all the fern fronds off the main stem.

4. Begin the layering process with four 19" fern fronds inserted up through the bottom of the shelf and into the foam. Continue with the two 19" chickweed stems and the two 18" mums. Insert the longest barba bode sprigs among the flowers and ferns.

5. Continue inserting and layering the pieces, building the waterfall to curve over the front of the shelf, angling from left to right. Cut the cabbage stem to 3" and insert into the foam center angled upward. Use the ribbon to make a puffy bow (see page 4) with a center loop, two 5" loops, and two 20" tails. Attach it to a wood pick and insert into the foam front.

6. Insert the shortest flowers, fern fronds and barba bode around the cabbage, angling away from it. Attach a wire loop hanger to the back.

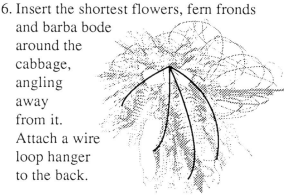

1. Remove the wheels from the wagon and paint them red. Spray the wagon blue and let all pieces dry. Spray the wagon with sealer. When dry, put the wheels back on the wagon.

2. Glue the soaked foam into the liner, then glue the liner in the wagon. Insert galax leaves around the edge of the wagon to hide the foam.

3. Cut the ribbon in half. Wrap one half around the bear's neck and tie into a bow. Glue him sitting on the edge of the wagon. Wire the wagon handle to the bear's left paw. Use the other ribbon half to tie the wagon handle into the left paw; allow one tail to drape downward. Coil the other tail along the front of the wagon, attaching one end and the center to a wood pick; insert the picks into the foam as shown.

4. Cut three white stock to these lengths: 21", 16" and 13". Insert them upright in the left end of the wagon. Cut five iris to these lengths: 18",15", 13", 11" and 8". Insert upright into the foam near the bear.

5. Spray the orientalis red. Insert four in a cluster in front of the iris and four in front of the stock. Spray the lace coral red. Pinch the stem end of each and attach to a pick; insert them into the left end of the foam to extend over the wagon edge.

6. Cut an 8" button mum sprig and insert between the iris and stock. Insert 3"-5" mum sprigs in front of the first, stair-stepping them down toward the front of the wagon.

7. Cut seven eucalyptus leaves off the stem, each with a 1"-2" stem. Insert the largest into the foam between the iris and bear, positioning it to extend horizontally forward. Continue inserting the leaves in the same manner, stacking them over each other and gradually using the smaller leaves. To hold the pavé look, use a dab of cool melt glue to attach each leaf to the last one.

8. Tuck tufts of moss among all the stems to hide the foam. Insert more clusters of eucalyptus behind the flowers to add depth to the arrangement.

TEDDY BEAR AND WAGON

vegetative style with the parallelism technique, fresh flowers
photo on page 42

wood wagon (from Walnut Hollow)
3 stems of white stock
5 stems of Dutch iris
9 stems of natural orientalis (from Schuster's of Texas)
3 stems of yellow button chrysanthemums
1 branch of eucalyptus
2 pieces of natural lace coral (from Colorado Evergreen Imports, Inc.)
16-18 galax leaves
sheet moss
one 8" beige teddy bear
3 yards of ⁵⁄₈" wide red satin ribbon
bright blue and bright red spray paints
gloss spray sealer
plastic liner to fit the wagon
floral foam for fresh flowers, soaked in water
18-gauge wire
4" long wired wood picks
low temperature glue gun and sticks

Designer Tip

• When attaching satin ribbon to a project, be sure to wire it to a wood pick and wrap with floral tape; when it is inserted into the foam, the ribbon will not become wet.

TEDDY BEAR AND WAGON
by Rich Salvaggio, AIFD, aaf

WOODLAND DESIGN
by Teresa Nelson

WOODLAND DESIGN
vegetative style, silk flowers
photo on page 43

18"x11" TWIGS™ door crown
7 stems of satin anemones, various colors
*   with 2" wide blossoms*
2 stems of yellow silk wild tanzia, each
*   with five 2" wide clusters of ¹/₄" wide*
*   fuzzy blossoms*
3 stems of blue silk forget-me-nots, each
*   with 3 sprigs of ten ¹/₂" wide blossoms*
*   and many 12" grass strands*
1 stem of fuchsia silk forsythia with 9
*   sprigs of three 1" wide blossoms*
9" long birch tube
3 stems of brown dried mushroom flowers,
*   each with one 3" wide mushroom*
3 oz. of green preserved tree fern
3" long mauve mushroom bird
8"x4"x3" block of floral foam for silks
¹/₄ oz. of sheet moss
U-shaped floral pins
30-gauge wire
hot glue gun and sticks

1. Cut the floral foam into two 8"x1¹/₂"x1¹/₂"; cover with moss in several places and wire the foam to the horizontal bar of the twig door crown.
2. Cut a 15" forget-me-not stem. Insert upright into the foam, just slightly left of center. Cut a 11" stem; insert it just left of the first stem. Cut a 9" stem, insert in front of both of the other stems.
3. Cut a 14" tanzia stem. Insert upright into the foam just right of the forget-me-nots. Cut the other tanzia stem into one 6" and an 11" sprig. Insert the 11" sprig to the right of the 14" tanzia stem, then insert the 6" sprig in front of both.
4. Cut 16" fern stems and insert behind the tallest forget-me-nots and tanzias. Cut 13" sprigs and insert behind the shorter tanzia stem and to the left of the forget-me-not at the back.
5. Cut the forsythia into a 12", 11", 8" and 5" sprig. Insert the 12" just left of the forget-me-not, with the 10" beside it, the 8" to the left of that one, and the 5" to the left of that one, right in a row, upright. Bend the flower sprigs so they look natural and fill in any empty areas.
6. Cut the anemones to 4"-9" lengths. Insert a 4" and 9" length to extend over the end of the twig crown. Insert a 5" length just to the right of the tanzia. Fill in the empty area between these anemones with the remaining 6"-8" anemones, spacing the colors equally.
7. Cut the bark lengthwise, splitting it completely through. Cut it again to make 5" wide pieces; break off the edges to make them uneven.
8. On the back of each bark piece glue two U-shaped floral pins to each piece, angling into the foam; let dry. When the glue is set, apply glue to the pins and push them into the foam, positioning the bark pieces to completely cover the foam.
9. Tuck tufts of moss among the stems to cover any exposed foam.
10. Cut the remaining tree fern into 5"-9" sprigs. Insert the 9" sprigs near the tallest flowers at each end, then insert the 5" sprigs along the front, between flower stems. Be sure to fill any empty spaces with the tree fern. Save a few 5" sprigs for later.
11. Cut the stems on each mushroom flower to 3", then insert 2 mushroom flowers at the center, just above the bark to extend over the front of the bark. Insert the third one 2" away from the first two, also extending over the edge of the bark. Glue the bird to the bark left of the two mushroom flowers. Fill any empty areas with tree fern. Make sure that all of the foam is covered with moss.
12. Attach a wire loop hanger to the back.

1. Cut the bottom from the cage and the hanger off the top. Invert the large tray. Cut a 2"x2"x2" block of foam into a dome; soak it and glue to the tray near one end. Place the cage over the foam and glue to the tray. Glue the small tray right side up at the right front of the cage. Soak foam and glue into the container.

2. Glue a small handful of moss to the upper left of the bird cage, then glue the bird among the moss.

3. Insert a galax leaf horizontally into the front of the foam near the left end of the small tray. Insert two wood picks just above the leaf, then glue a tuft of moss over the picks. Glue the bird to the moss so it is supported by the two picks. Insert more galax leaves around the front of the small tray to extend over the edge.

4. Insert galax leaves around the edge of the foam inside the cage. Attach the stem of the smilax garland to a wood pick and insert into the left side of the cage foam. Bring the garland out through the cage side, around the front, back through the cage at the front right corner and behind the bird, extending right of the tray. Pin it behind the bird.

5. Insert a 11" and a 7" tall rose into the cage foam, extending upright. Insert 6"–8" heather sprigs around the roses, angled away from them. Insert 5"–6" ming sprigs around the back of the foam to cover it.

6. Insert five roses into the tray foam, extending upright and stair-stepping from 4" to 16" in height. Insert two more angled over the right end of the tray.

7. Cut and insert 8"–18" heather stems into the tray to follow the asymmetrical triangle shape already established by the roses. Repeat with the Queen Anne's lace, filling the center areas.

BIRD CAGE

interpretative landscape style, fresh flowers
photo on page 46

6 ¹/₂"x6 ¹/₂"x19" twig bird cage
one 3" and one 4" blue/white mushroom bird
9 stems of pink bridal roses
6 stems of Queen Anne's lace
5 stems of pink heather
one 36" long smilax garland
1 stem of ming fern
1 bunch of galax leaves
sheet moss
one 10"x4¹/₂" white plastic tray
one 8"x3¹/₂" white plastic tray
floral foam for fresh flowers
U-shaped floral pins
4" long wood picks
hot glue gun and sticks

Designer Tips:
• When using roses in an arrangement leave some of the upper foliage; be sure what <u>is</u> left does not interfere with the established line.
• Using roses in various stages of openness makes arrangements look more natural.

BIRDCAGE
by Rich Salvaggio, AIFD, aaf

TWIG CRESCENT
by Teresa Nelson

TWIG CRESCENT

landscape style, silk flowers
photo on page 47

18" wide TWIGS™ arch
2 stems of pink silk roses, each with six
   1¹/₂" wide blossoms, 3 buds and many
   leaves
2 stems of green silk boxwood, each with
   eight 5"-9" sprigs of ³/₄" long leaves and
   yellow buds
3 stems of white silk gypso spray, each with
   8 sprigs of four ¹/₄" wide blossoms and 3
   buds
2 stems of pink silk wild heather, each with
   six 5"-8" sprigs of many ¹/₄" wide
   blossoms
¹/₄ oz. of sheet moss
2¹/₄ yards of 1¹/₂" wide pink floral print
   sheer ribbon
6" of 24-gauge wire
hot glue gun and sticks

1. Cut 6-7 twigs, that don't show, from the back of the arch and set aside.
2. Cut an 18" rose stem; curve, and insert into the twigs to extend to the end of the upper twigs. Cut the second stem into three 6"-8" sprigs; insert over the first stem near the center of the cresent. Arrange the blossoms among the twigs so that they look like they are climbing them.
3. Cut each boxwood into 8 sprigs. Insert in a cluster, as if they were a single plant, at the bottom of the crescent.
4. Cut each gypso stem into a 4-sprig spray and 4 individual sprigs. Glue two 4-sprig sprays behind the boxwood to extend upward. Glue the remaining sprigs evenly spaced around those two. Curve the blossoms to extend among the roses and down among the boxwood.
5. Cut a 3-sprig spray off one wild heather stem and glue near the center of the crescent, arranging it to climb among the roses. Cut the remaining heather into individual sprigs; glue them into a clump just to the right of the boxwood. Curve them among the boxwood, gypso spray and down among the twigs.
6. Insert 4 twigs from step 1 among the roses, down close to the center of the crescent. Insert the remaining twigs among the boxwood and heather.
7. Use the ribbon to make a puffy bow (see page 4) with a center loop, six 3" loops, a 4" and a 19" tail. Glue at the lower left; tuck the longer tail among the upper twigs and the shorter tail among the lower twigs.
8. Find the spot on the back of the crescent to place the hanger, so that it hangs straight. Attach a wire loop hanger to the back.

1. Invert the large saucer on the table and glue the other clay pots and saucer on it. Insert small liners into the two larger clay pots. Insert the soaked foam into the liners.

2. Make a $3^1/_2$" ribbon loop with a 5" and a 6" streamer and glue to hold; glue them into the small saucer to extend right. Glue the votive candle into the saucer over the ribbon ends. Wrap the remaining ribbon around a paint can to coil it. Cut a 14" length; glue one end to the right side of the small pot, angle it down and forward, then glue the other end to the lower edge of the large saucer. Repeat on the other side, attaching one end to the large pot and the other end to the large saucer edge; trim excess.

3. Insert two 15" ivy stems into the left side of the large pot. Insert a 6" stem angled right in the large pot and one extending horizontally right in the small pot.

4. Cut a gerbera to 8"; place wire on each side of it and floral tape to the end of the stem. Insert the stem into the small pot to extend horizontally right. Repeat with a 5" stem and insert left of the first. Insert a 3" gerbera at the front of the small pot, making sure the flame does not touch it.

5. Cut the snapdragons to these lengths: one19", one 15" and one 12". Insert them to extend upright in the center of the large pot with the tips bending left. Insert a 3" gerbera into the large pot just left of the snapdragon stems.

6. Cut a 16" stem of wax flowers and insert just right of the snapdragons. Cut a 9" sprig and insert just under the horizontal gerbera. Cut the remaining sprigs to 4"-7" lengths; insert them around the flowers in the large pot and tuck three around the flowers in the small pot.

7. Cut one mum to 8" and curve it (see Designer Tip, right); insert under the horizontal daisy at the right. Insert a 4" mum in front of it, then insert a 6" and a 4" mum into the large pot, angled left. Cut the remaining mums off the main stem and insert them at the front of the large pot right of the gerbera; these are terraced in the design and for success, begin with the shortest stem first.

8. Insert a 25" willow twig to extend upward in the large pot. Insert a 15" twig just left of it and another 15" twig into the small pot, curving over the edge.

TERRA COTTA SAUCER

interpretive garden style, fresh flowers
photo on page 50

13" wide round terra cotta saucer
round clay pots: one 5"x6", one 4"x5"
3"x1$^1/_2$" round clay saucer
3 stems of white snapdragons
2-3 stems of variegated ivy
4 stems of apple blossom gerbera daisies
3 stems of mauve wax flowers
1 stem of white button chrysanthemums
one 45" branch of curly willow with 3 sprigs
white votive candle
2$^1/_2$ yards of 1$^1/_2$" wide bronze tissue wired
   Bedford Bendable™ ribbon
floral foam for fresh flowers, soaked in water
floral tape
willow twigs: one 25" long, two 15" long
30-gauge wire, spray paint can, liners to fit
   the clay pots ,hot glue gun and sticks

Designer Tip

• Light the candle while working on the design. This allows you to make sure a flower won't interfere with the flame, and it's easier to light the candle later. If you can feel the heat on your finger as you are inserting stems, the flower will not last long in that position.

• To curve a mum, insert a 24-gauge wire up the stem and through the top of the flower. Bend the wire end into a hook and carefully pull it back down into the flower petals to disappear. Now gently curve the stem.

TERRA COTTA SAUCER
by Rich Salvaggio, AIFD, aaf

WREATH WITH HYDRANGEAS
by Teresa Nelson

WREATH WITH HYDRANGEAS

garden style, silk flowers
photo on page 51

18" twisted birch wreath
3 stems of blue silk hydrangea, each with a
    5" wide blossom cluster
5 stems of pink/yellow silk roses, each with
    a 2¹/₂" and a 2" wide blossom
1 stem of white/yellow silk narcissus, with
    three 10" sprigs of nine 1¹/₂" wide
    blossoms
1 green silk ivy bush with two 26" and two
    20" branches of 1"-2" wide leaves
¹/₂ oz. of natural dried rice grass
24-gauge wire
hot glue gun and sticks

1. Untwist two 24"-28" birch branches from the wreath. Place one on the right side and wire it around the lower front of the wreath. Repeat on the left side, and where the two branches cross in the front, wire them to secure.

2. Cut the branches from the ivy. Wire a 26" branch up the left side of the wreath and over the top. Repeat with the 20" branch on the outside of the wreath at the left. Wire a 20" branch to the wreath front, beginning at the lower left side and curving around the bottom of the wreath. Wire the last 26" branch from the left side around the front of the branches which were wired in step 1.

3. Cut the hydrangea to 12", 17" and 22". Wire them to extend up the left front of the wreath. Refer to the photo for placement.

4. Cut a rose stem to 10" and one to 8". Cut the remaining stems into 5"-6" single flower sprigs. Glue the 10" and 8" stems upright into the wreath, just right of the hydrangeas. The two upper hydrangeas should curve over the top of the roses. Glue the 5"-6" rose sprigs in front of the stems angling forward, left and right.

5. Cut a 10" narcissus sprig off the stem and glue near the 8" rose. Cut the remaining narcissus sprigs to 5"-6". Glue them evenly spaced among the shorter roses.

6. Cut the rice grass into 6"-14" sprigs and glue evenly spaced among the lower flowers. Glue any leftover silk leaves to fill any empty spaces.

7. Attach a wire loop hanger to the back.

ST. NICHOLAS ARRANGEMENT

crescent with intersecting vertical style with the framing technique, fresh flowers
photo on page 54

14" tall St. Nicholas figurine
3 cone/spruce/apple picks
3 stems of white stock
3 stems of white larkspur
black square plastic container
gold Deco-Lace™ spray paint
3 oz. of gold dried tango leaf (from
    International Floral Fashions)
1 oz. of burgundy dried ming fern
1 bunch of galax leaves
2 yards of gold spaghetti wired Bedford
    Bendable™ ribbon
4" long wired wood pick
floral foam for fresh flowers, soaked in
    water
low temperature glue gun and sticks

1. Spray the container with gold Deco-Lace™ and let dry. Glue the soaked foam into the container. Insert a large galax leaf into each corner of the foam to extend outward, then insert a smaller leaf over it.

2. Insert the three cone picks in a cluster in the front corner of the foam. Square the stem of a 19" long larkspur and attach to a wood pick; insert it into the left of the foam angled outward. Repeat with a 16" larkspur stem, inserting it horizontally at the right.

3. Strip most of the lower leaves off a 22" stock stem and insert it upright in the center of the foam. Repeat with a 16", a 14" and a 12" stem.

4. Insert the 8"–12" budded laterals from the larkspur stem near the blooming larkspur stems, echoing the lines of the arrangement. Insert a 12" larkspur stem at 45° angle left of the stock stems. Repeat with a 12" and an 8" stem on the left side.

5. Insert three 13"–15" tango leaf stems near each long larkspur stem, then insert one just left of the stock stems.

6. Cut the ming fern into 4"–6" sprigs. Insert among the lower flowers and picks to add depth to the arrangement.

7. Coil the ribbon into six 4"–6" concentric circles, securing the circles with the ribbon end. Attach the circles to a wood pick and insert into the foam to angle left and encircle the upper cone pick.

ST. NICHOLAS ARRANGEMENT
by Rich Salvaggio, AIFD, aaf

FRENCH HORN
by Teresa Nelson

FRENCH HORN
crescent style used to frame the cluster, silk flowers
photo on page 55

20"x14" pewter-look French horn
*1¼ yards of 2½" wide mauve/green brocade
   ribbon*
*1 stem of vinyl angel pine with twenty-one 6"
   sprigs*
*2 stems of mauve silk wild roses, each with
   four 1½"-3" wide blossoms*
*3 stems of pink silk wild blackberries, each
   with 8 sprigs of four ¼"-⅜" wide berries*
3 oz. of 16"-22" long birch branches
30-gauge wire
8" of 24-gauge wire (for the bow)
glue gun and sticks

1. Cut the pine into two 10" branches, each
   with 10-11 sprigs. Wire onto the horn
   end to end with the center area at the lower
   left (note the horn hangs slightly off-
   center).

2. Cut the rose stems to 14" long; wire them
   end to end over the pine branches. Pull ten
   twigs and set aside for step 4. Bundle the
   remaining twigs, positioning them at
   varying heights. Wire the bundle to the
   horn angled across the crescent established
   with the pine and roses.

3. Use the ribbon to make a puffy bow (see
   page 4) with a center loop, two 4" loops
   and 8" tails. Glue it over the bundle as
   shown. Cut each of two berry stems into
   two 10" sprigs; glue two evenly spaced
   into the pine on each side of the bow. Cut
   the remaining berry stem into one 8" and
   four 6" sprigs. Glue the 8" sprig to extend
   upward among the twigs; glue the 6" sprigs
   around the bow.

4. Glue the twigs from step 2 evenly spaced
   among the pine and roses.

5. Determine the location of the hanger to
   ensure the design hangs straight. Attach a
   wire loop hanger at this point.

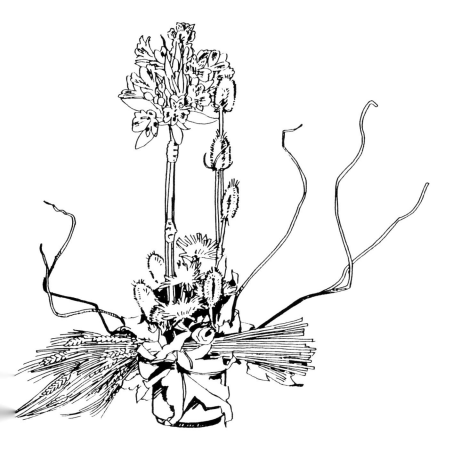

AUTUMN ARRANGEMENT

banding technique, fresh flowers
photo on page 58

4"x6" tall beige ceramic container
brown spray paint, sponge
floral foam for fresh flowers, soaked in
   water
4"–6" wide brown dried maple leaves
4 oz. of bleached dried wheat
3 stems of rosario alstromeria
3 oz. of mauve dried teasel
3 stems of white spider pom pom
   chrysanthemums
two 26" stems of curly willow
1 yard of gold spaghetti Bedford
   Bendable™ ribbon
sheet moss
cellophane tape
low temperature glue gun and sticks
hot glue gun and sticks

Designer Tip:
• If the glue does not hold a leaf on the container, attach a small piece of cellophane tape to the container. Then glue the leaf to the tape; it will stick without a problem.

1. Use a low temperature glue gun to temporarily attach three or four 4" wide maple leaves around the outside of the container. Spray brown paint onto a damp sponge. Gently dab around each leaf, stenciling the outline onto the container.
2. Glue the soaked foam into the container.
3. Hot glue three larger maple leaves onto the container, partially hiding the stencilled design. This adds depth to the container.
4. Hold all the wheat at varying heights and wrap with the ribbon, twisting the ends at the back to secure. Glue the bundle horizontally across the front of the container; use tape if necessary (see Designer Tip, left).
5. Hold all three 22"–24" alstromeria stems together and wrap with the ribbon just under the lowest blossom; wrap the ribbon around the stems three times, twisting the ends at the back to secure. Band them twice more evenly spaced down the stems. Insert them upright in the foam, just left of the center.
6. Hold three teasel stems at varying heights with the tallest at 21" and band together under the lowest head. Hold another stem in front of the first three and band it to them. Insert the stems just right of the alstromeria stems.
7. Insert maple leaves around the container rim, angling upward in back to pull the look of the container up into the arrangement. Tuck sheet moss among the leaves to hide the foam.
8. Beginning with a 7" mum, insert five stems between the alstromeria and teasel, stair-stepping them down toward the front of the container. Cut three 3"–6" teasel stems and insert into the foam just left of the alstromeria.
9. Cut a 26" willow stem and insert in the right foam, angled upward between the wheat stems and the longest teasel. Cut a 22" stem; insert it into the left foam, angled upward.

AUTUMN BANDED ARRANGEMENT
by Rich Salvaggio, AIFD, aaf

LADDER WITH DRIED
FLOWERS
by Teresa Nelson

LADDER WITH DRIED FLOWERS

clustering technique, silk flowers

photo on page 59

18" tall TWIGS™ ladder
1 oz. of natual dried orientalis
1 oz. of burgundy dried foxtail
2 oz. of navy dried hill flowers
2 oz. of burgundy dried starburst flowers
1 oz. of mauve dried pearly everlasting
*   flowers*
2¹/₂ yards of 1¹/₂" wide burgundy/brown
*   flowered sheer ribbon*
30-gauge wire
three 2"-2¹/₂" dried pomegranates
1 stem of burgundy/green silk berries with a
*   10" section of ¹/₄" wide berries and 1"*
*   leaves*
hot glue gun and sticks

1. Cut the orientalis into 13"-22" sprigs. Arrange them into a cluster, with the longest sprigs near the back of the cluster and the shortest sprigs near the front. Wrap with wire to secure and then wrap the wire around the left vertical bar of the ladder.

2. Repeat with the foxtail, cutting 9"-20" sprigs and arranging it in the same manner. Tie it left of the orientalis.

3. Cut 10"-14" sprigs of hill flowers, arrange them in a cluster. Wrap with wire to secure and then attach to the ladder located just right of the orientalis.

4. Cut the starburst into 5"-10" sprigs. Arrange and wrap them into a cluster as the orientalis in step 1. Attach the cluster in front of the blue hill flowers. Secure the cluster to the ladder bar with wire.

5. Cut the pearly everlastings into 3¹/₂"-8" sprigs. Arrange in a cluster and attach to the right vertical bar of the ladder.

6. Cut a 3" sprig of berries off the berry stem and set aside. Cut the remaining cluster to 8" and wire it over the pearly everlasting stems, allowing the section of berries to curve to the right of the pearly everlastings and up over the top. Wire the remaining sprig to extend downward and angled left over the top of the pearly everlasting stems.

7. Cut a 5" length of ribbon, wrap it around the left vertical bar of the ladder, over the top of the stems and tie into a knot; trim the tails off. Repeat on the right vertical bar of the ladder.

8. Use the ribbon to make a puffy bow (see page 4) with a center loop, six 3" loops, a 9" and a 30" tail. Glue over the ribbon on the left vertical bar with the short tail angled left. Pull the right tail to the right vertical bar, and glue it over the ribbon, allowing the tails to angle to the right and dangle down below. Knot each ribbon end. Pull some berries on the right vertical bar down to cover the glued ribbon. Cut the stems (if any) off of the pomegranate. Glue two above the bow and one angled to the right below the bow. Attach a wire loop hanger to the upper horizontal bar of the ladder.

1. Spray the sleigh red, let dry, then spray lightly with gold. Stain each reindeer; wipe to obtain the desired darkness. Lightly spray each reindeer with gold, allowing stain to show through. Spray the sleigh and reindeer with sealer.

2. Cut a 26" ribbon length; loop and glue it along the lower front of the sleigh. Make a 1½" long ribbon loop and glue over the 26" ribbon end near the sleigh front. Cut two 14" and two 12" ribbon lengths. Glue one of each around each reindeer's neck as shown.

3. Glue a silk holly sprig at each glued area on the sleigh ribbon. Glue a sprig at the glued areas on the reindeer ribbons.

4. Insert 7–9 galax leaves around the foam to hide the liner, aiming the leaves at the front downward.

5. Establish the "C" curve in the design using two lily buds. Cut one to 13", then wire to a wood pick. Dip just the pick tip into glue and insert it into the foam at the right end of the sleigh. Repeat with a 15" lily at the left end.

6. Cut two open lily blossoms with 4" stems and insert at the front of the design. Glue a wood pick into the stem of each gold ball and insert three in a cluster left of the open lilies. Insert balsam sprigs around the balls and open lilies to hide the foam.

7. To establish the vertical line in the design, insert a 19" Queen Anne's lace stem slightly left of the foam center. Insert a 14" and a 10" stem in front of the first lace stem. Insert 13", 9½" and 7" monte casino stems in a similar line just right of the lace stems.

8. Insert a 19" curly willow branch into the left side near the lily bud. Repeat with a 23" branch on the right, then bring the end of each together above the lace and wrap with a 1" length of ribbon.

9. Hold together five strands of bear grass, all facing the same direction, and attach a wood pick. Repeat with five more strands; insert one bunch into the foam on each side of the lily bud.

SLEIGH & REINDEER

negative/positive space element with the framing technique, fresh flowers
photo on page 62

12"x6"x7" wood sleigh with plastic liner
two 7"x10" wood reindeer
2 stems of white Casablanca lilies, each with a bud and an open blossom
4 stems of Queen Anne's lace
2 branches of curly willow
10 strands of bear grass
1 stem of ming fern
2½ yards of ³/₈" wide gold mesh ribbon
red and metallic gold spray paints
gloss spray sealer
4" long wired wood picks
fruitwood spray stain, clean cloth
floral foam for fresh flowers, soaked in water
balsam sprigs
2 stems of monte casino
5 sprigs of silk holly, each with three 1" long leaves, ½" berries and two 1" cones
1 bunch of galax leaves
four 2"wide gold balls
low temperature glue gun and sticks

10. Attach a wood pick to the last gold ball; insert it near the right end of the arrangement. To carry the gold up into the arrangement, wrap each of three areas of the willow with a 3" ribbon length. Hide the foam with sprigs of ming fern, balsam, and lace flowers.

SLEIGH & REINDEER
by Rich Salvaggio, AIFD, aaf

HEART WREATH
by Teresa Nelson

HEART WREATH

negative/positive space elements, silk flowers
photo on page 63

18"x15" twig heart wreath
4 yards of purple/green wire-edged ribbon
4 stems of purple silk daisies, each with three
*   9" sprigs of three 1"-1¹/₂" wide blossoms*
3 stems of blue silk China spray, each with 4
*   branches of three 4"-7" sprigs of two ¹/₂"*
*   wide blossoms and buds*
1 green silk geranium bush with 6 sprigs of
*   four 2³/₄" wide leaves*
2 stems of white silk Scottish heather, each
*   with 4 branches of three 5"-9" feathery*
*   sprigs*
2 oz. of green dried isolepsis
24-gauge wire
hot glue gun and sticks

1. Cut all the sprigs off the geranium bush; set one aside. Glue five evenly spaced along the lower right side of the wreath, three angled upward and two downward.
2. Use the ribbon to make a puffy bow (see page 4) with a center loop, two 3" loops, an 11" and a 43" tail. Glue to the upper left of the heart; loop and weave the long tail across the wreath to the point between the angled stems on the lower right. Glue the tail over this spot with 10" extending below the wreath. Use the remaining ribbon to make another puffy bow with a center loop, six 3" loops, a 6" and an 8" tail. Glue to the lower right over the tail.
3. Cut a daisy stem into 3"-4" sprigs; glue them evenly spaced around the upper bow. Cut the leaves off the geranium sprig from step 1 and glue evenly spaced around the upper bow. Cut the remaining daisies into 4"-5" sprigs; glue among the geranium leaves in the lower area, angled as the leaves.
4. Cut ten 3"-4" heather sprigs from one stem and glue evenly spaced among the flowers around the upper bow. Cut the remaining heather into 5"-9" sprigs and glue them evenly spaced among the lower flowers.
5. Cut one China spray into twelve 4"-7" sprigs; glue eight among the upper flowers and the rest around the lower bow. Cut each of the other two stems into four branches and glue them evenly spaced among the lower flowers, angling in the same directions.
6. Cut the upper 6"-7" of an isolepsis tuft off and glue in a cluster among the flowers. Repeat to glue clusters evenly spaced among all the flowers. Attach a wire loop hanger on the back.